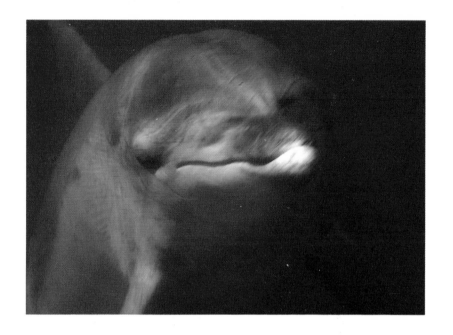

Waiting for Billy

MARTIN JACKA

ORCHARD BOOKS · NEW YORK

That's my grandpa over there by his boat. And that's Bib with him. She's a funny little dog. She's scared of the water, but all the same she goes out every day in the boat. I think she must like Grandpa a lot.

My grandpa doesn't go boating for fun. It's part of his job. He tows racehorses through the water.

Grandpa says swimming is very good exercise for horses. It makes their legs stronger so that they can gallop faster on the racetrack.

I bet Bib's skinny little legs would get stronger, too, if she went swimming. But Grandpa says Bib won't even put her nose in the water.

Just look at Grandpa's boat! All the paint has
peeled off. Mom says it's the shabbiest boat
on the river, but Grandpa won't paint it. He
says the horses like the boat. He says they
trust the-boat-that-hasn't-any-paint.

I wish I were out there with Grandpa and Bib in the-boat-that-hasn't-any-paint. The water is warm and the sun is out, which means it's going to be one of Grandpa's lucky days—one of the days when Billy comes to play.

Billy is a wild bottle-nosed dolphin.

He's lived in the estuary, where the sea meets the river, with some other dolphins all his life, which is probably why he isn't frightened of the fishermen and the boats that travel up and down the river.

Grandpa first met Billy about five years ago. The little dolphin was with his mother and father, but he seemed to be having trouble swimming. Grandpa helped him until he could swim on his own. The older dolphins left the river later, but the little one stayed, and Grandpa named him Billy.

Grandpa says Billy is one of the family. He says Billy waits for him behind an old ship named *Accolade*. Then, as soon as he hears Bib's barking and the put-put-putter of Grandpa's motorboat, he appears, rolling over on his side, blowing water spray at Grandpa and Bib, leaping out of the water,

not once,

but two, three, four, and five times!

Once Bib became so excited she forgot she was afraid of the sea and jumped into the water—for the first time ever—to swim with Billy.

She didn't like it much!

Sometimes Billy goes off for a few minutes to
visit the fishermen on the river.

When he comes back to Grandpa and Bib, he does something really amazing, something Grandpa says he has never seen another dolphin do.

Billy plays with the horses!

He jumps over them!

Dodges in and out!

Grandpa says the first time Billy did this, the horses were frightened. Perhaps they thought he was a shark. But now the horses are used to Billy and like his company, even if he does tease them sometimes.

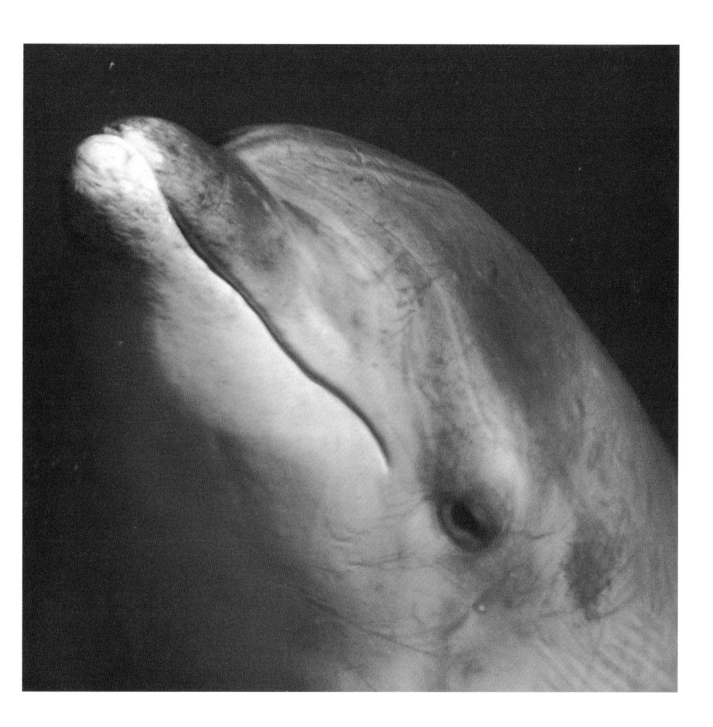

Once, when Grandpa took his friend Sam's dog out in the boat, the dog jumped into the water, too. Grandpa says it was wonderful seeing a horse and a dog and a dolphin all swimming together. It is one of his precious memories.

But now Billy is gone. Last summer a fleet of ships came into our port, and when they left, Billy and some of the other dolphins left, too. They followed the ships out toward the open sea, and they didn't come back.

It's strange, but some of the horses seem to hesitate these days before they go in the river for their early morning swim.

Grandpa says perhaps they are waiting for Billy.

But Grandpa's not waiting. He's glad Billy is
out there, somewhere in the ocean.

He says Billy will be having a great time with
the other wild dolphins. And right now, he is
probably leaping, not once, but two, three,
four, and five times in the air!

For Sandy Sandford and Bib

Copyright © 1990 by Martin Jacka
First American Edition 1991 published by Orchard Books. First published in Australia by Omnibus Books.

Orchard Books, A division of Franklin Watts, Inc., 387 Park Avenue South, New York, NY 10016

Manufactured in the United States of America. Printed by General Offset Company, Inc. Bound by Horowitz/Rae. Book design by Mina Greenstein. The text of this book is set in 18 pt. Plantin. The illustrations are full-color photographs. 10 9 8 7 6 5 4 3 2 1

Library of Congress Cataloging-in-Publication Data
Jacka, Martin. Waiting for Billy / Martin Jacka.—1st American ed. p. cm.
"First published by Omnibus Books, Australia"—T.p. verso. Summary: With his dog, a man exercises racehorses in the water and they are often joined by Billy, a bottle-nosed dolphin.
ISBN 0-531-05933-2. ISBN 0-531-08533-3 (lib.)
1. Dolphins—Anecdotes—Juvenile literature. 2. Race horses—Anecdotes—Juvenile literature. 3. Dogs—Anecdotes—Juvenile literature. [1. Dolphins—Anecdotes. 2. Horses—Anecdotes. 3. Dogs—Anecdotes.]
I. Title QL737.C432J28 1991 599.5'3—dc20 90-7957